D1366872

by Victor Gentle and Janet Perry

Gareth Stevens Publishing
A WORLD ALMANAC EDUCATION GROUP COMPANY

Please visit our web site at: www.garethstevens.com
For a free color catalog describing Gareth Stevens Publishing's
list of high-quality books and multimedia programs,
call 1-800-542-2595 or fax your request to (414) 332-3567.

Library of Congress Cataloging-in-Publication Data

Gentle, Victor.
    Tigers / by Victor Gentle and Janet Perry.
        p. cm. — (Big cats: an imagination library series)
    Includes bibliographical references and index.
    Summary: Introduces tigers and their behavior and habitat.
    ISBN 0-8368-3029-6 (lib. bdg.)
    1. Tigers—Juvenile literature. [1. Tigers.] I. Perry, Janet, 1960- II. Title.
QL737.C23G49 2002
599.756—dc21   2001049697

First published in 2002 by
Gareth Stevens Publishing
A World Almanac Education Group Company
330 West Olive Street, Suite 100
Milwaukee, WI 53212 USA

Text: Victor Gentle and Janet Perry
Page layout: Victor Gentle, Janet Perry, and Tammy Gruenewald
Cover design: Tammy Gruenewald
Series editor: Catherine Gardner
Picture Researcher: Diane Laska-Swanke

Photo credits: Cover, p. 13 © Tom & Pat Leeson; pp. 5, 11, 15, 17 © Alan & Sandy Carey;
pp. 7, 9, 19 (main) © E. A. Kuttapan/BBC Natural History Unit; p. 19 (inset) © Michael K.
Nichols/NGS Image Collection; p. 21 © David Welling/BBC Natural History Unit

Printed in the United States of America

1 2 3 4 5 6 7 8 9 06 05 04 03 02

Front cover: A fine Bengal tiger wades powerfully
through a tropical marshland. Unlike most other
cats — big or small — tigers seem to love the water.

TABLE OF CONTENTS

Words that appear in the glossary are printed in **boldface** type the first time they occur in the text.

JUST KIDDING AROUND

Slowly, the young tiger creeps through the low bushes. Now, it stands still. Its stripes blend into the shadows. Its **prey** does not sense the danger. The tiger creeps even closer. With a rush, the tiger leaps and lands on the back of its prey — its mother.

By playing with its mother, the **cub** learns to hunt. It is too young to hunt alone. The cub will need lots of practice before it is ready for real prey.

Mother tigers need lots of patience. Their bouncy cubs use them for target practice, over and over and over.

CUBHOOD

The cub was born only weeks ago. The cub and its **littermates** were tiny, blind, and helpless. The **litter** may have as many as seven cubs. The mother tiger fiercely guards her cubs from **predators** and even other tigers.

Their first food is mother's milk. After eight weeks, she might bring them some meat. Another twelve weeks, and the cubs tag along after her. First she takes them to her kills. Later they go on hunting field trips with her to watch and learn.

Mothers change **dens** for safety, carrying their cubs there one by one. They do this when they think their den has been discovered by a predator.

EARNING THEIR STRIPES

By the time the cubs are one year old, they hunt with their mother most of the time. The cubs are too small to catch big prey and too clumsy to catch much small prey. They need their mother's kills to stay well fed. Slowly and surely, they learn.

The cubs are ready to leave home when they are two years old. Young male tigers often travel far from their mothers to set up a **territory**. The females usually stay nearby, sometimes taking part of their mother's territory.

Cubs go hunting with their mother. They watch everything she does for many months. Then, the cubs practice on mice, insects — and each other.

WHAT'S FOR DINNER?

What's for dinner depends on where a tiger lives. Bengal tigers live in areas with lots of deer, so deer are a favorite food for Bengal tigers. They also eat monkeys, cattle, wild pigs, crocodiles, birds, and other prey.

Fewer deer live in the places where Siberian tigers live. But there are plenty of wild pigs and moose, so Siberian tigers hunt mostly wild pigs and moose. They enjoy other prey, too, including bears, deer, marsh hens, and **lynxes**.

A Siberian tiger **marks** a tree. Siberians are the biggest wild cats. The smallest tigers, Sumatrans, weigh only half as much as Siberian tigers.

STALKING STYLE

Most animals can outrun tigers — if they get the chance. In fact, tigers make a kill only about once in 15 tries! The tiger's secret is to get close enough without being noticed.

Silently a tiger **stalks** its prey. Often it takes a few steps, freezes, takes a few more steps, and then freezes again. The final charge must be short and swift. Suddenly, the tiger leaps and snatches its prey in its bone-crushing jaws.

Well hidden in the grass, a tiger stalks its prey. Each time a stalking tiger stops, it crouches low, ready to spring.

MALES AND FEMALES

Male tigers never share hunting grounds with other males. But a male's territory may cover parts of territories that belong to females. Except when it is time to **mate**, males steer clear of females.

When a female is pregnant, she will not welcome the male. She protects her cubs from all predators, especially other tigers. Some males play with and feed their own cubs. Males may kill other tiger cubs, however — sometimes even their own.

A mother tiger with cubs will fiercely guard her territory. Both males and females mark their territories to warn other tigers to stay away.

TIGER TURF

Tigers live in many **habitats**. Some tigers live in hot, dry forests. Others live in hot, wet jungles. Still other tigers survive in cold northern forests or on snow-covered mountains.

At one time, hundreds of thousands of tigers lived in Asia, from Siberia and China west to Turkey and south through India. Today, fewer than 8,000 tigers may be alive.

Not so long ago, there were eight kinds of tigers. Three kinds of tigers have become **extinct** in the last 50 years. The remaining five kinds are **endangered**.

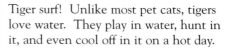

Tiger surf! Unlike most pet cats, tigers love water. They play in water, hunt in it, and even cool off in it on a hot day.

TIGERS ON THE RUN

Humans are the worst enemies tigers have ever had. A hundred years ago, 235 million people and 40,000 Bengal tigers lived in India. Today, India has a billion people and fewer than 4,000 tigers.

By cutting forests to make farms, humans crowd out tigers and their prey. Some farmers poison tigers to protect their herds. Hungry villagers steal the animals that tigers have killed. **Poachers** still kill tigers to sell their skins and body parts — even where tigers are protected!

In the small picture, a Russian officer shows a tiger skin that has been taken from poachers. In the big picture, the skins are right where they ought to be!

SAVING THE TIGERS

Of the five kinds of wild tigers left, three kinds are very close to becoming extinct. In southern China, all the wild tigers may die, even though humans are trying to help them survive. There are just too few tigers.

People must make room for tigers and their prey in wild places. People must stop poaching and learn that if we do not protect tigers, we will lose these awesome animals forever — and know that we destroyed them.

Each tiger's skin has a unique pattern, like a fingerprint. No other tiger in the world is quite like this beauty. Let's hope it survives.

MORE TO READ AND VIEW

Books (Nonfiction)   *Big Cats* (series). Victor Gentle and Janet Perry (Gareth Stevens)
Fast, Strong and Striped. Moira Butterfield (Raintree Steck-Vaughn)
Mammals, the Hunters. Christopher O'Toole and John Stidworthy
  (Facts on File)
Save the Tiger. Jill Bailey (Steck-Vaughn)
Tiger, Tiger, Growing Up. Joan Hewett (Clarion)

Books (Activity)   *Drawing the Big Cats.* Paul Frame (Franklin Watts)
Tiger Math. Ann Whitehead Nagda and Cindy Bickel (Henry Holt)

Books (Fiction)   *Tiger.* Judy Allen (Candlewick)
Tiger Watch. Jan Wahl (Harcourt Brace Jovanovich)
Who Is the Beast? Keith Baker (Harcourt Brace Jovanovich)

Videos (Nonfiction)   *Jungle Animals.* (Dorling Kindersley)
Land of the Tiger. (National Geographic)

PLACES TO VISIT, WRITE, OR CALL

Tigers live at the following zoos. Call or write to the zoos to find out about their tigers and their plans to preserve tigers in the wild. Better yet, go see the tigers, person to cat!

Lincoln Park Zoo
2200 North Cannon Drive
Chicago, IL 60614
(312) 742-2000

Honolulu Zoo
151 Kapahulu Avenue
Honolulu, HI 96815
(808) 926-3191

Cincinnati Zoo & Botanical Gardens
3400 Vine Street
Cincinnati, OH 45220
1-800-94-HIPPO

Los Angeles Zoo
5333 Zoo Drive
Los Angeles, CA 90027-1498
(323) 644-6400

WEB SITES

Web sites change frequently, but we believe the following web sites are going to last. You also can use a good search engine, such as **Yahooligans!** [*www.yahooligans.com*] or **Google** [*www.google.com*], to find more information about tigers, other big cats around the world, and their homes. Some keywords that will help you do this are: *tigers, Siberian tigers, Bengal tigers, cats, Asian wildlife*, and *endangered species*.

www.yahooligans.com
Yahooligans! is a great research tool. It has a lot of information and plenty to do. Under Science and Nature, click on Animals and then click on The Big Picture: Animals. From there, you can try Animal Videos, Endangered Animals, Animal Bytes, BBC Animals, or Natural History Notebooks and search for information on tigers, jungles, mountains, and Indonesian or Asian wildlife.

www.pbs.org/kratts/
Visit *Kratt's World.* Go to the Creature World map and click on a continent to see what other animals live side by side with tigers.

www.super-kids.com
Super-Kids will take you to games and pictures of big cats, along with other information about big cats. Start by clicking on Animals. Then, try Africa, Monkeys, Tigers, or Zoos.

www.5tigers.org
At 5 *Tigers*, you can listen to tiger noises. Or, click on KIDS to play games, answer questions, and see awesome tiger pictures.

www.kidsplanet.org
Kids' Planet by Defenders of Wildlife has many things to do. Click on Games for fun, or the Web of Life Story to learn how cats fit into our world, or Defend It to find out how to help stop people from killing tigers.

www.nationalgeographic.com/features/ 97/cats/
National Geographic has a really cool game that lets you design the perfect predator.

www.nhm.org/cats/
The Natural History Museum of Los Angeles County has a really great exhibit called *Cats! Mild to Wild.* Click on Biology, and you will find how cats are built, how they use their claws, teeth, legs, and voices — and more!

www.vrd.org/locator/subject.shtml#science
Do you have more questions about tigers? Try *Ask an Expert.* This site has scientists and naturalists who will help you find out whatever you need to know.

GLOSSARY

You can find these words on the pages listed. Reading a word in a sentence helps you understand it even better.

cub (KUHB) — a big cat's baby 4, 6, 8, 14

dens (DENZ) — places where animals give birth, hide their cubs, and sleep 6

endangered (en-DAYN-jurd) — at risk of becoming extinct or dying out 16

extinct (ex-TINKT) — with none of its kind alive any more 16, 20

habitats (HAB-uh-tats) — natural places where a type of animal lives that gives it enough food and shelter 16

litter (LIT-ur) — a group of cubs born at the same time to the same mother 6

littermates (LIT-ur MAYTS) — a cub's brothers and sisters born at the same time 6

lynxes (LINGKS-es) — medium-sized wild cats with short tails, spotted fur, and tufted ear tips 10

marks (MARKS) — leaves a scent or scratches to warn other animals that a territory already belongs to a tiger 10, 14

mate (MAYT) — come together to make babies 14

poachers (POHCH-erz) — people who hunt and kill animals illegally 18, 20

predators (PRED-uh-turs) — animals that hunt other animals for food 6, 14

prey (PRAY) — animals that are hunted by other animals for food 4, 8, 10, 12, 18, 20

stalks (STAWKS) — to quietly follow prey 12

territory (TER-uh-tor-ee) — an area of land that an animal (or group of animals) marks out as its hunting ground 8, 14

INDEX

24